Scholastic Clifford THE BIG RED DOG™ BIG Coloring and Activity Book

Clifford's Funny Follies

Modern Publishing
A Division of Unisystems, Inc.
New York, New York 10022

Printed in the U.S.A.
Series UPC: 49585

Clifford and Friends

Around and Around We Go!

A Bone for Everyone!

1. HOME SWEET HOME

Connect the dots from 1 to 33 to see where T-Bone lives.

See Answers

2. A GIFT FOR CLIFFORD

Emily Elizabeth loves Clifford! Color the picture using the code in the box.

Clifford's Best Pals

Hi, Clifford!

A Clifford Kiss

T-Bone and Cleo

Clifford and his friends wait for their owners after school.

START

FINISH

3. TREASURE HUNT
Clifford, Cleo, T-Bone, and Emily Elizabeth are searching for treasure! Help them by following the correct path through the maze.

See Answers

4. CLEO'S NEW FRIEND

Cleo made a new friend in the park today!
Color in all of the spaces with a bone to see her
new friend.

See Answers

A Great Catch

Playing Dress-Up

Riding Home to Clifford

Hi, T-Bone!

5. GIVE ME A C!

Clifford's and Cleo's names begin with the letter C. Circle all of the other things on this page that begin with the letter C. Then color the pictures.

See Answers

An Ice-Cream Cone Big Enough for Clifford!

A Day in the Park

6. CLIFFORD AND COMPANY

Clifford's friends come in all shapes and sizes! Circle the biggest dog. Put a square around the smallest dog. Underline the medium-sized dog. Then color the pictures.

See Answers

School is out!

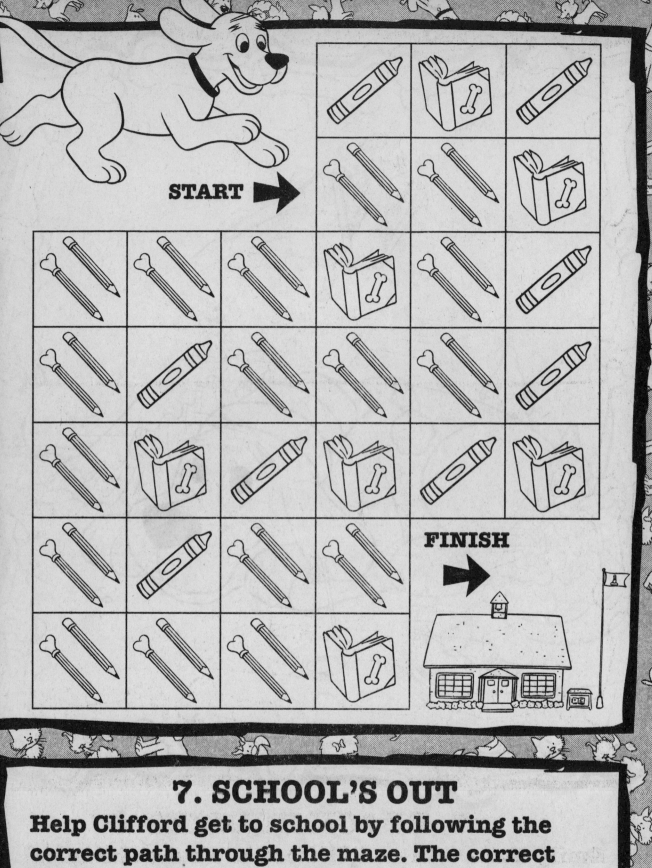

START ➡

FINISH ➡

7. SCHOOL'S OUT

Help Clifford get to school by following the correct path through the maze. The correct path is made up of pencils only. Move up, down, and across only.

See Answers

Splish-splashing

8. BEACH BUDDIES

Emily Elizabeth and Clifford are beach buddies!
Can you find and circle five things in the bottom
picture that are not in the top picture?

See Answers

Fun in the Park

9. LET'S GO TO THE LIBRARY!

It's time for a trip to the library! Draw a picture of your favorite Birdwell Island friends going to the library. Draw yourself in the picture, too!

10. LOOK-ALIKES

Two of these pictures of Charley look exactly alike. Can you find and circle them?

See Answers

Emily Elizabeth loves Clifford!

11. OUT OF PLACE
Emily Elizabeth adds the finishing touch—
with a little help from Clifford! There are five
things that do not belong in this scene. Find
and circle them. Then color the picture.

See Answers

Going to the Groomer

T-Bone has a visitor!

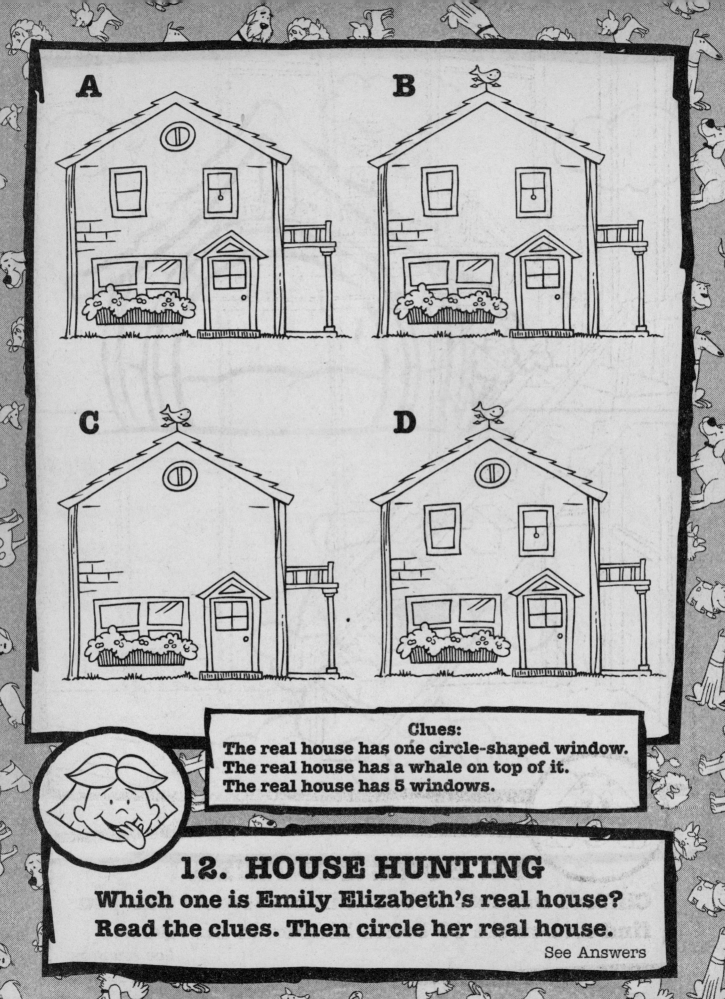

A

B

C

D

Clues:
The real house has one circle-shaped window.
The real house has a whale on top of it.
The real house has 5 windows.

12. HOUSE HUNTING
Which one is Emily Elizabeth's real house?
Read the clues. Then circle her real house.

See Answers

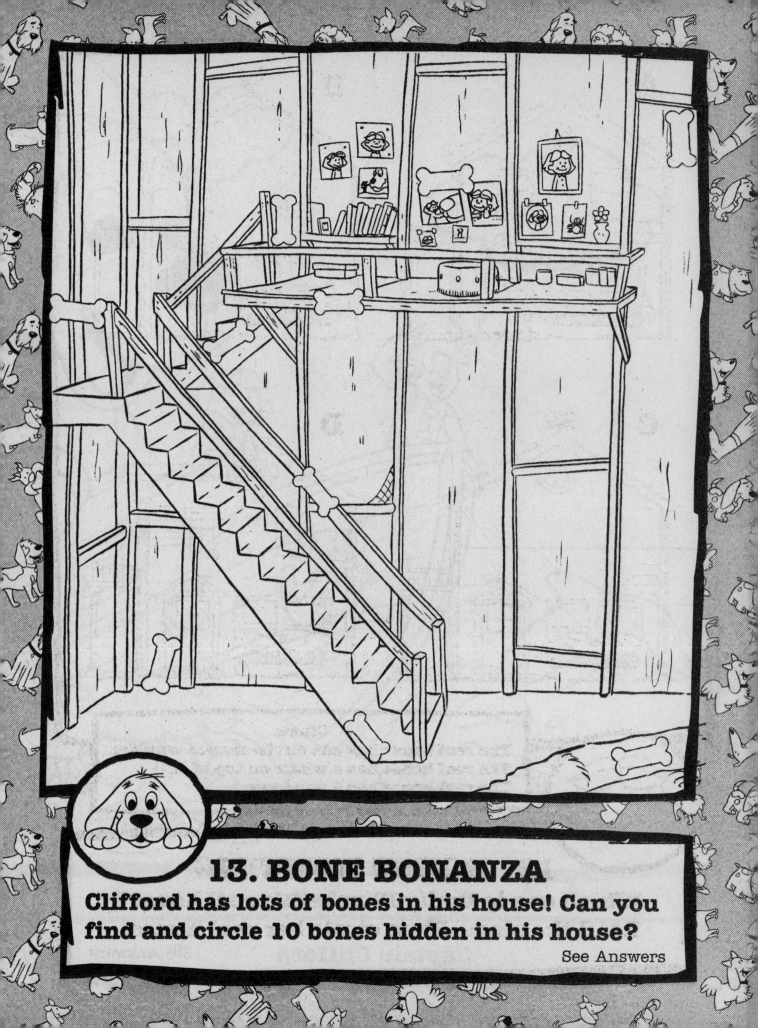

13. BONE BONANZA

Clifford has lots of bones in his house! Can you find and circle 10 bones hidden in his house?

See Answers

Captain Clifford

18. SEASIDE SCENE

T-Bone meets lots of new friends at the beach! Look at the pictures on this page. Circle the creature that he would not see at the beach.

See Answers

On the Pier

A.

B.

C.

D.

17. MAIL MIX-UP

Mr. Carson has to get to the Post Office to report for duty! But which one is the real Post Office? It is the one that is different from the others. Circle it.

See Answers

A Winning Team

Safe Skaters

Dive in, Cleo!

16. CHARLEY'S PLACE

This is Charley's houseboat. Draw Charley and Emily Elizabeth on the boat. Draw yourself in the picture, too!

START

FINISH

15. SAMUEL'S FISH AND CHIPS

It's time for Samuel to open up his shop! Help him get there by following the correct path through the maze.

See Answers

Hide and Seek

Heading Back to Birdwell Island

A.

B.

C.

D.

14. CLEO'S PLACE
Cleo played all day long! Now it is time for her to go home. Which house do you think is hers? Circle it.

See Answers

T-Bone is shy.

Clifford is a part of the playground!

Clifford helps out!

A Lift from a Friend

19. STRIKE UP THE BAND!

Emily Elizabeth and Charley want to start a band! Look at the objects on this page. Circle all of the things they will need for the band. Then color the pictures.

See Answers

Clifford Camps Out

20. NOW YOU SEE IT, NOW YOU DON'T

Three of these people are wearing something that one of the people is not wearing. Can you find and circle the person who is different? Then color the pictures.

See Answers

21. TASTY TREAT
What's this yummy treat that Clifford has sniffed out? Connect the dots from 1 to 30 to find out.

See Answers

A Day at the Beach

A Work of Art

A New Friend

22. WINTER FUN

It's a cold winter's day on Birdwell Island!
Circle all of the things that Emily Elizabeth
will use on such a cold day.

See Answers

Time for a Snooze

A Playful Autumn Day

Clifford is a dog to look up to!

1=RED
2=YELLOW
3=GREEN
4=BROWN
5=BLUE

23. CATCH, CLIFFORD!
Clifford is about to make a great catch! Color
the picture using the code in the box.

24. TIME FOR WORK

Everyone has a special job to do. Match each person on the right with the place where he or she works on the left.

See Answers

Emily Elizabeth and Friends

Soccer Star

START

FINISH

25. BIRTHDAY BOY
Clifford smells a yummy birthday cake! Help him find it by following the correct path through the maze. The correct path is made up of crayons only. Move up, down, and across only.

See Answers

Look what I found!

Come back to Birdwell Island soon!

Answers

1.

3.

4.

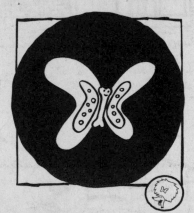

5.

6.

7.

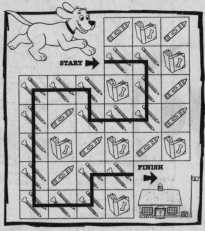

8.

10.

Answers

11.

15.

12.

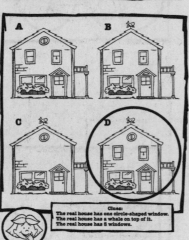

Clues:
The real house has one circle-shaped window.
The real house has a whale on top of it.
The real house has 5 windows.

17.

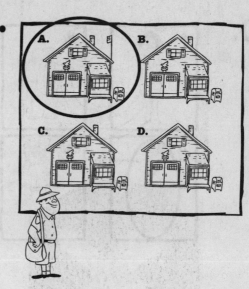

13.

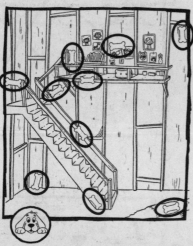

18.

14.

Answers

19.

22.

20.

24.

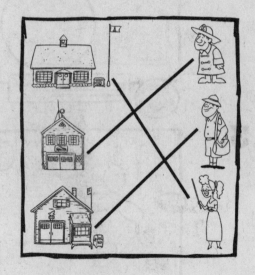

21.

25.